Life Well Designed

A Journal to Create Your Best Self

First Printing: 2018

ISBN 9781729203989

Seashells and Storytime
Freeport, Maine
Stacey@seashellsandstorytime.com
www.seashellsandstorytime.com

THIS JOURNAL BELONGS TO:

You only have one life...

Isn't yours worth living to the fullest?

Life is busy, overwhelming and just plain hard sometimes. We can embrace the challenges or we can complain about them. We can learn from our failures, accept the unexpected and choose to be happy or choose to be discouraged and defeated. The fact that you are using this journal tells me that you are choosing to put your health and well-being first. You are choosing happy! Way to go!

Wellness is more than eating right and exercising (which are equally important). It's taking care of both your mind and body, prioritizing your self-care and showing up each and every day.

This journal will help you define and track your dreams, affirmations, and goals, find your WHY, prioritize your health, and design a life where you are excited to wake up each morning!

Where to Start

Dream...

Let's start by digging really deep. On the first page make a list of everything you want in life if time and money were not a factor. Dream big and small. Where do you want to see yourself in one year, in five years and in ten? How do you want to make a difference in your life, your children's lives and the lives of others? What hobbies do you want to pursue or charities do you want to help? Do you have aspiring career goals or dreams to retire? What does your perfect home look like? Do you want to travel? Don't stop yet! Keep going...write down everything you want out of life.

Find Your Why...

What are your best qualities? Write down all your strengths, work experience and qualities that make you an amazing human being. Feeling stuck? Ask friends and family for help. They see you from a different perspective and will have great insight into your best qualities.

Next, circle two or three of the most unique qualities that you love about yourself.

Consider your best qualities and your dreams to find your WHY. What is your purpose? What motivates and drives you? What makes you feel fulfilled? What gives you energy? What do you love to talk about?

Thinking about your dreams, your best qualities and the questions above write a one or two sentence statement that defines your WHY and your purpose in life. This may take time to work through and can change over time. There are note pages at the end of this journal if you need extra space to write.

Write Affirmations...

Now that you've defined your dreams it's time to put them into action! Affirmations are statements that you read over and over and over again until they penetrate into your subconscious mind. They reprogram your mind to shut negativity out and let positivity in.

Affirmations should address the things you desire in life - your self-image, your career, and your relationships, as well as the tangible things you want in life if they are important to you - a new house, a new car or a vacation you're dreaming about.

The more often you repeat your affirmations, the faster you will be able to rewire your brain. Notice the triggers that are causing negative thoughts and practice replacing them with an affirmation. This takes a lot of time and patience, however, with consistency you will slowly see your mindset and energy levels change.

When writing affirmations stick to the following guidelines:

- Keep them brief, but specific.
- Start with I am.
- Use the present tense as if you have already achieved your goal.
- Use action words, emotions and feelings.
- Keep them positive. Always affirm what you want, not what you don't want.

Define Your Goals...

A dream is just a wish without a plan. Goal setting is crucial to fulfilling your purpose, your success and your happiness.

We suggest setting specific goals in the following areas of your life:

- Personal Development
- Health/Fitness
- Career
- Spiritual/Religious
- Family/Relationships
- Financial
- Fun

When developing your goals, they need to be S.M.A.R.T. – specific, measurable, achievable, relevant and time sensitive. For example, it's not enough to say you want to lose weight or be healthy. Instead, your goal should be "I will exercise 5 times per week for 30 minutes per day." Or "I will wake up at 5:30 am to practice my morning routine 6 days a week." The more detailed and clear your goals are, the more your subconscious mind will work to achieve them.

Read...

Dr. Seuss says it best - "The more that you read the more things you will know, the more that you learn, the more places you'll go." This quote doesn't just apply to kids - reading personal development books will help you grow and develop. Keep a log of books you want to read and make it part of your daily routine.

If you are struggling with any of the steps above, reading will help you find the answers.

Looking for book recommendations? Check out
www.seashellsandstorytime.com/book-recommendations for inspiration.

Self-Care...

Last but certainly not least - do not forget your self-care. Self-care is not simply indulging in spa appointments, nights out, or coffee dates. Self-care is having the discipline to prioritize your physical and mental health and wellness. Utilizing this journal is the first step in your self-care. Make sure to incorporate daily wellness routines and take time for yourself each day. And don't forget to indulge now and then too. You deserve it! We've included some ideas to help you get started and space to add some of your own.

What are you waiting for?

Now that you know exactly what you're working towards it's time to jump in! Each day you have the opportunity to track your progress and hold yourself accountable to achieving your goals and taking care of your mind and body.

If you don't already have routines and habits to incorporate your wellness goals into your daily life - it's time to start. We suggest creating a morning routine to focus on your wellness. You will be amazed at the energy and patience you have during your day when you start by focusing on YOU.

The daily journal pages include space for you to track your affirmations, meditation, reading, self-care, goals, healthy eating, water consumption and exercise. These are all important pieces of your health and well-being. Practicing gratitude also has a significant impact on your wellness and mindset. Write down three things you are grateful for each day and use the additional space to journal about any thoughts you are having.

Hold yourself accountable for tracking your progress and journaling each day and you will see a huge improvement in your health, energy levels and mindset!

Let's get started...

My Dreams and
Aspirations

"The biggest adventure you can take is to live the life
of your dreams." - Oprah Winfrey

My Dreams and Aspirations

CONTINUED...

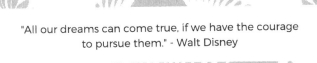

"All our dreams can come true, if we have the courage
to pursue them." - Walt Disney

My Best Qualities

"I figured that if I said it enough, I would convince the world that I really was the greatest." - Muhammad Ali

MY WHY

MY AFFIRMATIONS

GOALS

Goal:

Action Steps:

Completed by Date:

Goal:

Action Steps:

Completed by Date:

Goal:

Action Steps:

Completed by Date:

GOALS

Goal:

Action Steps:

Completed by Date:

Goal:

Action Steps:

Completed by Date:

Goal:

Action Steps:

Completed by Date:

GOALS

Goal:

Action Steps:

Completed by Date:

Goal:

Action Steps:

Completed by Date:

Goal:

Action Steps:

Completed by Date:

GOALS

Goal:

Action Steps:

Completed by Date:

Goal:

Action Steps:

Completed by Date:

Goal:

Action Steps:

Completed by Date:

What to Read

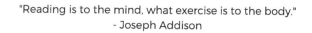

"Reading is to the mind, what exercise is to the body."
- Joseph Addison

Self-Care Ideas

- go for a walk
- take a bath/shower
- read a book/magazine
- meditate
- sleep-in
- date night
- girls/guys night out

- treat yourself to a pedicure
- go shopping
- watch a movie
- go to bed early
- journal
- go to the library
- grab a coffee

Self-care is not selfish

MAKING TODAY *Great!*

DATE: _____

AFFIRMATIONS ☐

MEDITATION ☐

READING ☐

SELF-CARE _____

CLOSER TO MY GOAL

_____

_____

_____

HEALTHY EATING

_____

_____

_____

WATER

EXERCISE

_____

I AM GRATEFUL

THOUGHTS

LIVE FOR TODAY. DREAM ABOUT TOMORROW. BE GRATEFUL. LAUGH.

MAKING TODAY *Great!*

DATE:

AFFIRMATIONS ☐

MEDITATION ☐

READING ☐

SELF-CARE

CLOSER TO MY GOAL

HEALTHY EATING

WATER ⊔⊔⊔⊔⊔⊔⊔

EXERCISE

I AM GRATEFUL

THOUGHTS

LIVE FOR TODAY. DREAM ABOUT TOMORROW. BE GRATEFUL. LAUGH.

MAKING TODAY *Great!*

DATE: _____

AFFIRMATIONS ☐

MEDITATION ☐

READING ☐

SELF-CARE _____

CLOSER TO MY GOAL

_____

_____

_____

HEALTHY EATING

_____

_____

_____

_____

WATER ⊔⊔⊔⊔ ⊔⊔⊔⊔

EXERCISE

_____

_____

I AM GRATEFUL

THOUGHTS

LIVE FOR TODAY. DREAM ABOUT TOMORROW. BE GRATEFUL. LAUGH.

MAKING TODAY *Great!*

DATE:

AFFIRMATIONS ☐

MEDITATION ☐

READING ☐

SELF-CARE

CLOSER TO MY GOAL

HEALTHY EATING

WATER ▽▽▽▽▽▽▽

EXERCISE

I AM GRATEFUL

THOUGHTS

LIVE FOR TODAY. DREAM ABOUT TOMORROW. BE GRATEFUL. LAUGH.

MAKING TODAY *Great!*

DATE: _____

AFFIRMATIONS ☐

MEDITATION ☐

READING ☐

SELF-CARE _____

CLOSER TO MY GOAL

_____

_____

_____

HEALTHY EATING

_____

_____

_____

_____

WATER ▯▯▯▯ ▯▯▯▯

EXERCISE

_____

_____

I AM GRATEFUL

THOUGHTS

LIVE FOR TODAY. DREAM ABOUT TOMORROW. BE GRATEFUL. LAUGH.

MAKING TODAY *Great!*

DATE:

AFFIRMATIONS ☐

MEDITATION ☐

READING ☐

SELF-CARE

CLOSER TO MY GOAL

HEALTHY EATING

WATER ⊔⊔⊔⊔⊔⊔⊔

EXERCISE

I AM GRATEFUL

THOUGHTS

LIVE FOR TODAY. DREAM ABOUT TOMORROW. BE GRATEFUL. LAUGH.

MAKING TODAY *Great!*

DATE: _____

AFFIRMATIONS ☐

MEDITATION ☐

READING ☐

SELF-CARE _____

CLOSER TO MY GOAL

_____

_____

HEALTHY EATING

_____

_____

_____

WATER 🥛🥛🥛🥛🥛🥛🥛

EXERCISE

_____

I AM GRATEFUL

THOUGHTS

MAKING TODAY *Great!*

DATE:

AFFIRMATIONS ☐

MEDITATION ☐

READING ☐

HEALTHY EATING

SELF-CARE

CLOSER TO MY GOAL

WATER 🥛🥛🥛🥛🥛🥛🥛

EXERCISE

I AM GRATEFUL

THOUGHTS

LIVE FOR TODAY. DREAM ABOUT TOMORROW. BE GRATEFUL. LAUGH.

MAKING TODAY *Great!*

DATE: _____

AFFIRMATIONS ☐

MEDITATION ☐

READING ☐

SELF-CARE _____

CLOSER TO MY GOAL

_____

_____

_____

HEALTHY EATING

_____

_____

_____

WATER ▽▽▽▽ ▽▽▽▽

EXERCISE

_____

I AM GRATEFUL

THOUGHTS

LIVE FOR TODAY. DREAM ABOUT TOMORROW. BE GRATEFUL. LAUGH.

MAKING TODAY *Great!*

DATE:

AFFIRMATIONS ☐

MEDITATION ☐

READING ☐

SELF-CARE

CLOSER TO MY GOAL

HEALTHY EATING

WATER ▽▽▽▽▽▽▽

EXERCISE

I AM GRATEFUL

THOUGHTS

LIVE FOR TODAY. DREAM ABOUT TOMORROW. BE GRATEFUL. LAUGH.

MAKING TODAY *Great!*

DATE: _____

AFFIRMATIONS ☐

MEDITATION ☐

READING ☐

SELF-CARE _____

CLOSER TO MY GOAL
_____
_____
_____

HEALTHY EATING
_____
_____
_____
_____

WATER 🥛🥛🥛🥛🥛🥛🥛🥛

EXERCISE
_____
_____

I AM GRATEFUL

THOUGHTS

LIVE FOR TODAY. DREAM ABOUT TOMORROW. BE GRATEFUL. LAUGH.

MAKING TODAY *Great!*

DATE:

AFFIRMATIONS ☐

MEDITATION ☐

READING ☐

SELF-CARE

CLOSER TO MY GOAL

HEALTHY EATING

WATER 🥤🥤🥤🥤🥤🥤🥤

EXERCISE

I AM GRATEFUL

THOUGHTS

MAKING TODAY *Great!*

DATE:

AFFIRMATIONS ☐

MEDITATION ☐

READING ☐

SELF-CARE

CLOSER TO MY GOAL

HEALTHY EATING

WATER ⊔⊔⊔⊔ ⊔⊔⊔

EXERCISE

I AM GRATEFUL

THOUGHTS

LIVE FOR TODAY. DREAM ABOUT TOMORROW. BE GRATEFUL. LAUGH.

MAKING TODAY *Great!*

DATE:

AFFIRMATIONS ☐

MEDITATION ☐

READING ☐

SELF-CARE

CLOSER TO MY GOAL

HEALTHY EATING

WATER 🥛🥛🥛🥛🥛🥛🥛

EXERCISE

I AM GRATEFUL

THOUGHTS

LIVE FOR TODAY. DREAM ABOUT TOMORROW. BE GRATEFUL. LAUGH.

MAKING TODAY *Great!*

DATE: _____

AFFIRMATIONS ☐

MEDITATION ☐

READING ☐

SELF-CARE _____

CLOSER TO MY GOAL

_____

_____

_____

HEALTHY EATING

_____

_____

_____

WATER 🥤🥤🥤🥤🥤🥤🥤

EXERCISE

_____

_____

I AM GRATEFUL

THOUGHTS

LIVE FOR TODAY. DREAM ABOUT TOMORROW. BE GRATEFUL. LAUGH.

MAKING TODAY *Great!*

DATE:

AFFIRMATIONS ☐

MEDITATION ☐

READING ☐

SELF-CARE

CLOSER TO MY GOAL

HEALTHY EATING

WATER ▽▽▽▽▽▽▽

EXERCISE

I AM GRATEFUL

THOUGHTS

LIVE FOR TODAY. DREAM ABOUT TOMORROW. BE GRATEFUL. LAUGH.

MAKING TODAY *Great!*

DATE: _____

AFFIRMATIONS ☐

MEDITATION ☐

READING ☐

SELF-CARE _____

CLOSER TO MY GOAL

_____

_____

_____

HEALTHY EATING

_____

_____

_____

WATER 🥛🥛🥛🥛🥛🥛🥛

EXERCISE

_____

I AM GRATEFUL

THOUGHTS

LIVE FOR TODAY. DREAM ABOUT TOMORROW. BE GRATEFUL. LAUGH.

MAKING TODAY *Great!*

DATE:

AFFIRMATIONS ☐

MEDITATION ☐

READING ☐

HEALTHY EATING

SELF-CARE

CLOSER TO MY GOAL

WATER 🥛🥛🥛🥛🥛🥛🥛

EXERCISE

I AM GRATEFUL

THOUGHTS

LIVE FOR TODAY. DREAM ABOUT TOMORROW. BE GRATEFUL. LAUGH.

MAKING TODAY *Great!*

DATE: _____

AFFIRMATIONS ☐

MEDITATION ☐

READING ☐

SELF-CARE

CLOSER TO MY GOAL

HEALTHY EATING

WATER 🥛🥛🥛🥛🥛🥛🥛

EXERCISE

I AM GRATEFUL

THOUGHTS

LIVE FOR TODAY. DREAM ABOUT TOMORROW. BE GRATEFUL. LAUGH.

MAKING TODAY *Great!*

DATE:

AFFIRMATIONS ☐

MEDITATION ☐

READING ☐

SELF-CARE

CLOSER TO MY GOAL

HEALTHY EATING

WATER 🥤🥤🥤🥤🥤🥤🥤

EXERCISE

I AM GRATEFUL

THOUGHTS

LIVE FOR TODAY. DREAM ABOUT TOMORROW. BE GRATEFUL. LAUGH.

MAKING TODAY *Great!*

DATE: _____

AFFIRMATIONS ☐

MEDITATION ☐

READING ☐

SELF-CARE _____

CLOSER TO MY GOAL

_____

_____

_____

HEALTHY EATING

_____

_____

_____

WATER ▽▽▽▽ ▽▽▽▽

EXERCISE

_____

_____

I AM GRATEFUL

THOUGHTS

LIVE FOR TODAY. DREAM ABOUT TOMORROW. BE GRATEFUL. LAUGH.

MAKING TODAY *Great!*

DATE:

AFFIRMATIONS ☐

MEDITATION ☐

READING ☐

SELF-CARE

CLOSER TO MY GOAL

HEALTHY EATING

WATER 🥤🥤🥤🥤🥤🥤🥤

EXERCISE

I AM GRATEFUL

THOUGHTS

MAKING TODAY *Great!*

DATE: _____

AFFIRMATIONS ☐

MEDITATION ☐

READING ☐

SELF-CARE _____

CLOSER TO MY GOAL
_____
_____
_____

HEALTHY EATING
_____
_____
_____
_____

WATER 🥤🥤🥤🥤🥤🥤🥤

EXERCISE
_____
_____

I AM GRATEFUL

THOUGHTS

LIVE FOR TODAY. DREAM ABOUT TOMORROW. BE GRATEFUL. LAUGH.

MAKING TODAY *Great!*

DATE:

AFFIRMATIONS ☐

MEDITATION ☐

READING ☐

SELF-CARE _____

CLOSER TO MY GOAL

_____

_____

HEALTHY EATING

_____

_____

_____

WATER ▽▽▽▽▽▽▽

EXERCISE

I AM GRATEFUL

THOUGHTS

LIVE FOR TODAY. DREAM ABOUT TOMORROW. BE GRATEFUL. LAUGH.

MAKING TODAY *Great!*

DATE: _____

AFFIRMATIONS ☐

MEDITATION ☐

READING ☐

SELF-CARE _____

CLOSER TO MY GOAL

_____

_____

_____

HEALTHY EATING

_____

_____

_____

_____

WATER ▽▽▽▽ ▽▽▽▽

EXERCISE

_____

_____

I AM GRATEFUL

THOUGHTS

LIVE FOR TODAY. DREAM ABOUT TOMORROW. BE GRATEFUL. LAUGH.

MAKING TODAY *Great!*

DATE:

AFFIRMATIONS ☐

MEDITATION ☐

READING ☐

SELF-CARE

CLOSER TO MY GOAL

HEALTHY EATING

WATER 🥛🥛🥛🥛🥛🥛🥛

EXERCISE

I AM GRATEFUL

THOUGHTS

MAKING TODAY *Great!*

DATE: _____

AFFIRMATIONS ☐

MEDITATION ☐

READING ☐

SELF-CARE

CLOSER TO MY GOAL

HEALTHY EATING

WATER

EXERCISE

I AM GRATEFUL

THOUGHTS

LIVE FOR TODAY. DREAM ABOUT TOMORROW. BE GRATEFUL. LAUGH.

MAKING TODAY *Great!*

DATE:

AFFIRMATIONS ☐

MEDITATION ☐

READING ☐

HEALTHY EATING

SELF-CARE

CLOSER TO MY GOAL

WATER 🥤🥤🥤🥤🥤🥤🥤🥤

EXERCISE

I AM GRATEFUL

THOUGHTS

LIVE FOR TODAY. DREAM ABOUT TOMORROW. BE GRATEFUL. LAUGH.

MAKING TODAY *Great!*

DATE: _____

AFFIRMATIONS ☐

MEDITATION ☐

READING ☐

SELF-CARE _____

CLOSER TO MY GOAL

_____

_____

_____

HEALTHY EATING

_____

_____

_____

_____

WATER ⊔⊔⊔⊔ ⊔⊔⊔

EXERCISE

_____

_____

I AM GRATEFUL

THOUGHTS

LIVE FOR TODAY. DREAM ABOUT TOMORROW. BE GRATEFUL. LAUGH.

MAKING TODAY *Great!*

DATE:

AFFIRMATIONS ☐

MEDITATION ☐

READING ☐

SELF-CARE

CLOSER TO MY GOAL

HEALTHY EATING

WATER 🥤🥤🥤🥤🥤🥤🥤

EXERCISE

I AM GRATEFUL

THOUGHTS

LIVE FOR TODAY. DREAM ABOUT TOMORROW. BE GRATEFUL. LAUGH.

MAKING TODAY *Great!*

DATE: _____

AFFIRMATIONS ☐

MEDITATION ☐

READING ☐

SELF-CARE

CLOSER TO MY GOAL

HEALTHY EATING

WATER 🥛🥛🥛🥛🥛🥛🥛

EXERCISE

I AM GRATEFUL

THOUGHTS

LIVE FOR TODAY. DREAM ABOUT TOMORROW. BE GRATEFUL. LAUGH.

MAKING TODAY *Great!*

DATE:

AFFIRMATIONS ☐

MEDITATION ☐

READING ☐

SELF-CARE

CLOSER TO MY GOAL

HEALTHY EATING

WATER 🥤🥤🥤🥤🥤🥤🥤

EXERCISE

I AM GRATEFUL

THOUGHTS

LIVE FOR TODAY. DREAM ABOUT TOMORROW. BE GRATEFUL. LAUGH.

MAKING TODAY *Great!*

DATE:

AFFIRMATIONS ☐

MEDITATION ☐

READING ☐

SELF-CARE

CLOSER TO MY GOAL

HEALTHY EATING

WATER 🥤🥤🥤🥤🥤🥤🥤

EXERCISE

I AM GRATEFUL

THOUGHTS

LIVE FOR TODAY. DREAM ABOUT TOMORROW. BE GRATEFUL. LAUGH.

MAKING TODAY *Great!*

DATE:

AFFIRMATIONS ☐

MEDITATION ☐

READING ☐

SELF-CARE _____

CLOSER TO MY GOAL

_____

_____

_____

HEALTHY EATING

WATER 🥛🥛🥛🥛🥛🥛🥛

EXERCISE

I AM GRATEFUL

THOUGHTS

LIVE FOR TODAY. DREAM ABOUT TOMORROW. BE GRATEFUL. LAUGH.

MAKING TODAY *Great!*

DATE: _____

AFFIRMATIONS ☐

MEDITATION ☐

READING ☐

SELF-CARE

CLOSER TO MY GOAL

HEALTHY EATING

WATER 🥛🥛🥛🥛🥛🥛🥛

EXERCISE

I AM GRATEFUL

THOUGHTS

LIVE FOR TODAY. DREAM ABOUT TOMORROW. BE GRATEFUL. LAUGH.

MAKING TODAY *Great!*

DATE:

AFFIRMATIONS ☐

MEDITATION ☐

READING ☐

SELF-CARE

CLOSER TO MY GOAL

HEALTHY EATING

WATER ⬜⬜⬜⬜⬜⬜⬜⬜

EXERCISE

I AM GRATEFUL

THOUGHTS

LIVE FOR TODAY. DREAM ABOUT TOMORROW. BE GRATEFUL. LAUGH.

MAKING TODAY *Great!*

DATE: _____

AFFIRMATIONS ☐

MEDITATION ☐

READING ☐

SELF-CARE

CLOSER TO MY GOAL

HEALTHY EATING

WATER 🥤🥤🥤🥤🥤🥤🥤

EXERCISE

I AM GRATEFUL

THOUGHTS

LIVE FOR TODAY. DREAM ABOUT TOMORROW. BE GRATEFUL. LAUGH.

MAKING TODAY *Great!*

DATE:

AFFIRMATIONS ☐

MEDITATION ☐

READING ☐

SELF-CARE

CLOSER TO MY GOAL

HEALTHY EATING

WATER ⊔⊔⊔⊔⊔⊔⊔

EXERCISE

I AM GRATEFUL

THOUGHTS

LIVE FOR TODAY. DREAM ABOUT TOMORROW. BE GRATEFUL. LAUGH.

MAKING TODAY *Great!*

DATE: _____

AFFIRMATIONS ☐

MEDITATION ☐

READING ☐

SELF-CARE _____

CLOSER TO MY GOAL

_____
_____
_____

HEALTHY EATING

_____
_____
_____

WATER 🥛🥛🥛🥛🥛🥛🥛

EXERCISE

_____
_____

I AM GRATEFUL

THOUGHTS

LIVE FOR TODAY. DREAM ABOUT TOMORROW. BE GRATEFUL. LAUGH.

MAKING TODAY *Great!*

DATE:

AFFIRMATIONS ☐

MEDITATION ☐

READING ☐

HEALTHY EATING

SELF-CARE

CLOSER TO MY GOAL

WATER ⌴⌴⌴⌴⌴⌴⌴

EXERCISE

I AM GRATEFUL

THOUGHTS

LIVE FOR TODAY. DREAM ABOUT TOMORROW. BE GRATEFUL. LAUGH.

MAKING TODAY *Great!*

DATE: _____

AFFIRMATIONS ☐

MEDITATION ☐

READING ☐

SELF-CARE

CLOSER TO MY GOAL

HEALTHY EATING

WATER

EXERCISE

I AM GRATEFUL

THOUGHTS

LIVE FOR TODAY. DREAM ABOUT TOMORROW. BE GRATEFUL. LAUGH.

MAKING TODAY *Great!*

DATE:

AFFIRMATIONS ☐

MEDITATION ☐

READING ☐

SELF-CARE

CLOSER TO MY GOAL

HEALTHY EATING

WATER ⊔⊔⊔⊔⊔⊔⊔

EXERCISE

I AM GRATEFUL

THOUGHTS

LIVE FOR TODAY. DREAM ABOUT TOMORROW. BE GRATEFUL. LAUGH.

MAKING TODAY *Great!*

DATE:

AFFIRMATIONS ☐

MEDITATION ☐

READING ☐

SELF-CARE

CLOSER TO MY GOAL

HEALTHY EATING

WATER 🥛🥛🥛🥛🥛🥛🥛

EXERCISE

I AM GRATEFUL

THOUGHTS

LIVE FOR TODAY. DREAM ABOUT TOMORROW. BE GRATEFUL. LAUGH.

MAKING TODAY *Great!*

DATE: _____

AFFIRMATIONS ☐

MEDITATION ☐

READING ☐

SELF-CARE _____

CLOSER TO MY GOAL

_____

_____

_____

HEALTHY EATING

_____

_____

_____

WATER

EXERCISE

_____

I AM GRATEFUL

THOUGHTS

LIVE FOR TODAY. DREAM ABOUT TOMORROW. BE GRATEFUL. LAUGH.

MAKING TODAY *Great!*

DATE:

AFFIRMATIONS ☐

MEDITATION ☐

READING ☐

SELF-CARE

CLOSER TO MY GOAL

HEALTHY EATING

WATER 🥛🥛🥛🥛🥛🥛🥛

EXERCISE

I AM GRATEFUL

THOUGHTS

LIVE FOR TODAY. DREAM ABOUT TOMORROW. BE GRATEFUL. LAUGH.

MAKING TODAY *Great!*

DATE: _____

AFFIRMATIONS ☐

MEDITATION ☐

READING ☐

HEALTHY EATING
_____
_____
_____
_____

SELF-CARE
_____

CLOSER TO MY GOAL

WATER 🥛🥛🥛🥛🥛🥛🥛
_____
_____
_____

EXERCISE
_____
_____

I AM GRATEFUL

THOUGHTS

LIVE FOR TODAY. DREAM ABOUT TOMORROW. BE GRATEFUL. LAUGH.

MAKING TODAY *Great!*

DATE:

AFFIRMATIONS ☐

MEDITATION ☐

READING ☐

SELF-CARE

CLOSER TO MY GOAL

HEALTHY EATING

WATER 🥛🥛🥛🥛🥛🥛🥛

EXERCISE

I AM GRATEFUL

THOUGHTS

LIVE FOR TODAY. DREAM ABOUT TOMORROW. BE GRATEFUL. LAUGH.

MAKING TODAY *Great!*

DATE: _____

AFFIRMATIONS ☐

MEDITATION ☐

READING ☐

SELF-CARE

CLOSER TO MY GOAL

HEALTHY EATING

WATER 🥤🥤🥤🥤🥤🥤🥤

EXERCISE

I AM GRATEFUL

THOUGHTS

LIVE FOR TODAY. DREAM ABOUT TOMORROW. BE GRATEFUL. LAUGH.

MAKING TODAY *Great!*

DATE:

AFFIRMATIONS ☐

MEDITATION ☐

READING ☐

SELF-CARE

CLOSER TO MY GOAL

HEALTHY EATING

WATER 🥛🥛🥛🥛🥛🥛🥛

EXERCISE

I AM GRATEFUL

THOUGHTS

LIVE FOR TODAY. DREAM ABOUT TOMORROW. BE GRATEFUL. LAUGH.

MAKING TODAY *Great!*

DATE: _____

AFFIRMATIONS ☐

MEDITATION ☐

READING ☐

SELF-CARE

CLOSER TO MY GOAL

HEALTHY EATING

WATER 🥛🥛🥛🥛🥛🥛🥛

EXERCISE

I AM GRATEFUL

THOUGHTS

LIVE FOR TODAY. DREAM ABOUT TOMORROW. BE GRATEFUL. LAUGH.

MAKING TODAY *Great!*

DATE:

AFFIRMATIONS ☐

MEDITATION ☐

READING ☐

SELF-CARE

CLOSER TO MY GOAL

HEALTHY EATING

WATER 🥛🥛🥛🥛🥛🥛🥛

EXERCISE

I AM GRATEFUL

THOUGHTS

LIVE FOR TODAY. DREAM ABOUT TOMORROW. BE GRATEFUL. LAUGH.

MAKING TODAY *Great!*

DATE: _____

AFFIRMATIONS ☐

MEDITATION ☐

READING ☐

SELF-CARE

CLOSER TO MY GOAL

HEALTHY EATING

WATER 🥛🥛🥛🥛🥛🥛🥛🥛

EXERCISE

I AM GRATEFUL

THOUGHTS

LIVE FOR TODAY. DREAM ABOUT TOMORROW. BE GRATEFUL. LAUGH.

MAKING TODAY *Great!*

DATE:

AFFIRMATIONS ☐

MEDITATION ☐

READING ☐

SELF-CARE

CLOSER TO MY GOAL

HEALTHY EATING

WATER ⛉⛉⛉⛉⛉⛉⛉⛉

EXERCISE

I AM GRATEFUL

THOUGHTS

MAKING TODAY *Great!*

DATE: _____

AFFIRMATIONS ☐

MEDITATION ☐

READING ☐

SELF-CARE _____

CLOSER TO MY GOAL

_____

_____

_____

HEALTHY EATING

_____

_____

_____

_____

WATER ⛆⛆⛆⛆⛆⛆⛆

EXERCISE

_____

_____

I AM GRATEFUL

THOUGHTS

LIVE FOR TODAY. DREAM ABOUT TOMORROW. BE GRATEFUL. LAUGH.

MAKING TODAY *Great!*

DATE:

AFFIRMATIONS ☐

MEDITATION ☐

READING ☐

SELF-CARE

CLOSER TO MY GOAL

HEALTHY EATING

WATER 🥤🥤🥤🥤🥤🥤🥤🥤

EXERCISE

I AM GRATEFUL

THOUGHTS

MAKING TODAY *Great!*

DATE: _____

AFFIRMATIONS ☐

MEDITATION ☐

READING ☐

SELF-CARE _____

CLOSER TO MY GOAL

_____

_____

_____

HEALTHY EATING

_____

_____

_____

_____

WATER ☐☐☐☐☐☐☐☐

EXERCISE

_____

_____

I AM GRATEFUL

THOUGHTS

LIVE FOR TODAY. DREAM ABOUT TOMORROW. BE GRATEFUL. LAUGH.

MAKING TODAY *Great!*

DATE:

AFFIRMATIONS ☐

MEDITATION ☐

READING ☐

SELF-CARE

CLOSER TO MY GOAL

HEALTHY EATING

WATER ▽▽▽▽▽▽▽

EXERCISE

I AM GRATEFUL

THOUGHTS

LIVE FOR TODAY. DREAM ABOUT TOMORROW. BE GRATEFUL. LAUGH.

MAKING TODAY *Great!*

DATE: _____

AFFIRMATIONS ☐

MEDITATION ☐

READING ☐

SELF-CARE

CLOSER TO MY GOAL

_____

_____

_____

HEALTHY EATING

_____

_____

_____

_____

WATER ᗡᗡᗡᗡᗡᗡᗡᗡ

EXERCISE

_____

I AM GRATEFUL

THOUGHTS

LIVE FOR TODAY. DREAM ABOUT TOMORROW. BE GRATEFUL. LAUGH.

MAKING TODAY *Great!*

DATE:

AFFIRMATIONS ☐

MEDITATION ☐

READING ☐

SELF-CARE

CLOSER TO MY GOAL

HEALTHY EATING

WATER 🥛🥛🥛🥛🥛🥛🥛🥛

EXERCISE

I AM GRATEFUL

THOUGHTS

LIVE FOR TODAY. DREAM ABOUT TOMORROW. BE GRATEFUL. LAUGH.

MAKING TODAY *Great!*

DATE: _____

AFFIRMATIONS ☐

MEDITATION ☐

READING ☐

SELF-CARE _____

CLOSER TO MY GOAL

_____

_____

_____

HEALTHY EATING

_____

_____

_____

_____

WATER ☐☐☐☐☐☐☐☐

EXERCISE

_____

_____

I AM GRATEFUL

THOUGHTS

LIVE FOR TODAY. DREAM ABOUT TOMORROW. BE GRATEFUL. LAUGH.

MAKING TODAY *Great!*

DATE:

AFFIRMATIONS ☐

MEDITATION ☐

READING ☐

SELF-CARE

CLOSER TO MY GOAL

HEALTHY EATING

WATER 🥛🥛🥛🥛🥛🥛🥛

EXERCISE

I AM GRATEFUL

THOUGHTS

LIVE FOR TODAY. DREAM ABOUT TOMORROW. BE GRATEFUL. LAUGH.

MAKING TODAY *Great!*

DATE: _____

AFFIRMATIONS ☐

MEDITATION ☐

READING ☐

HEALTHY EATING
_____
_____
_____

SELF-CARE

CLOSER TO MY GOAL
_____
_____
_____

WATER 🥛🥛🥛🥛🥛🥛🥛

EXERCISE
_____

I AM GRATEFUL

THOUGHTS

LIVE FOR TODAY. DREAM ABOUT TOMORROW. BE GRATEFUL. LAUGH.

MAKING TODAY *Great!*

DATE:

AFFIRMATIONS ☐

MEDITATION ☐

READING ☐

SELF-CARE

CLOSER TO MY GOAL

HEALTHY EATING

WATER ⬚⬚⬚⬚⬚⬚⬚

EXERCISE

I AM GRATEFUL

THOUGHTS

LIVE FOR TODAY. DREAM ABOUT TOMORROW. BE GRATEFUL. LAUGH.

MAKING TODAY *Great!*

DATE: _____

AFFIRMATIONS ☐

MEDITATION ☐

READING ☐

SELF-CARE

CLOSER TO MY GOAL

HEALTHY EATING

WATER

EXERCISE

I AM GRATEFUL

THOUGHTS

LIVE FOR TODAY. DREAM ABOUT TOMORROW. BE GRATEFUL. LAUGH.

MAKING TODAY *Great!*

DATE:

AFFIRMATIONS ☐

MEDITATION ☐

READING ☐

HEALTHY EATING

SELF-CARE

CLOSER TO MY GOAL

WATER 🥛🥛🥛🥛🥛🥛🥛

EXERCISE

I AM GRATEFUL

THOUGHTS

LIVE FOR TODAY. DREAM ABOUT TOMORROW. BE GRATEFUL. LAUGH.

MAKING TODAY *Great!*

DATE: _____

AFFIRMATIONS ☐

MEDITATION ☐

READING ☐

SELF-CARE _____

CLOSER TO MY GOAL

_____

_____

_____

HEALTHY EATING

_____

_____

_____

_____

WATER 🥤🥤🥤🥤🥤🥤🥤

EXERCISE

_____

_____

I AM GRATEFUL

THOUGHTS

LIVE FOR TODAY. DREAM ABOUT TOMORROW. BE GRATEFUL. LAUGH.

MAKING TODAY *Great!*

DATE:

AFFIRMATIONS ☐

MEDITATION ☐

READING ☐

SELF-CARE

CLOSER TO MY GOAL

HEALTHY EATING

WATER ▽▽▽▽ ▽▽▽

EXERCISE

I AM GRATEFUL

THOUGHTS

MAKING TODAY *Great!*

DATE: _____

AFFIRMATIONS ☐

MEDITATION ☐

READING ☐

SELF-CARE _____

CLOSER TO MY GOAL

_____

_____

_____

HEALTHY EATING

_____

_____

_____

_____

WATER ▭▭▭▭▭▭▭▭

EXERCISE

_____

_____

I AM GRATEFUL

THOUGHTS

LIVE FOR TODAY. DREAM ABOUT TOMORROW. BE GRATEFUL. LAUGH.

MAKING TODAY *Great!*

DATE:

AFFIRMATIONS ☐

MEDITATION ☐

READING ☐

SELF-CARE

CLOSER TO MY GOAL

HEALTHY EATING

WATER ⊔⊔⊔⊔ ⊔⊔⊔⊔

EXERCISE

I AM GRATEFUL

THOUGHTS

LIVE FOR TODAY. DREAM ABOUT TOMORROW. BE GRATEFUL. LAUGH.

MAKING TODAY *Great!*

DATE: _____

AFFIRMATIONS ☐

MEDITATION ☐

READING ☐

HEALTHY EATING
_____
_____
_____
_____

SELF-CARE _____

CLOSER TO MY GOAL
_____
_____
_____

WATER ▽▽▽▽ ▽▽▽▽

EXERCISE
_____
_____

I AM GRATEFUL

THOUGHTS

LIVE FOR TODAY. DREAM ABOUT TOMORROW. BE GRATEFUL. LAUGH.

MAKING TODAY *Great!*

DATE:

AFFIRMATIONS ☐

MEDITATION ☐

READING ☐

SELF-CARE

CLOSER TO MY GOAL

HEALTHY EATING

WATER 🥛🥛🥛🥛🥛🥛🥛

EXERCISE

I AM GRATEFUL

THOUGHTS

MAKING TODAY *Great!*

DATE: _____

AFFIRMATIONS ☐

MEDITATION ☐

READING ☐

SELF-CARE

CLOSER TO MY GOAL

HEALTHY EATING

WATER  🥤🥤🥤🥤🥤🥤🥤

EXERCISE

I AM GRATEFUL

THOUGHTS

LIVE FOR TODAY. DREAM ABOUT TOMORROW. BE GRATEFUL. LAUGH.

MAKING TODAY *Great!*

DATE:

AFFIRMATIONS ☐

MEDITATION ☐

READING ☐

SELF-CARE

CLOSER TO MY GOAL

HEALTHY EATING

WATER ⌷⌷⌷⌷⌷⌷⌷

EXERCISE

I AM GRATEFUL

THOUGHTS

LIVE FOR TODAY. DREAM ABOUT TOMORROW. BE GRATEFUL. LAUGH.

MAKING TODAY *Great!*

DATE: _____

AFFIRMATIONS ☐

MEDITATION ☐

READING ☐

SELF-CARE _____

CLOSER TO MY GOAL

_____

_____

_____

HEALTHY EATING

_____

_____

_____

_____

WATER 🥛🥛🥛🥛🥛🥛🥛🥛

EXERCISE

_____

_____

I AM GRATEFUL

THOUGHTS

LIVE FOR TODAY. DREAM ABOUT TOMORROW. BE GRATEFUL. LAUGH.

MAKING TODAY *Great!*

DATE:

AFFIRMATIONS ☐

MEDITATION ☐

READING ☐

SELF-CARE

CLOSER TO MY GOAL

HEALTHY EATING

WATER 🥛🥛🥛🥛🥛🥛🥛🥛

EXERCISE

I AM GRATEFUL

THOUGHTS

LIVE FOR TODAY. DREAM ABOUT TOMORROW. BE GRATEFUL. LAUGH.

MAKING TODAY *Great!*

DATE: _____

AFFIRMATIONS ☐

MEDITATION ☐

READING ☐

SELF-CARE _____

CLOSER TO MY GOAL

_____

_____

HEALTHY EATING

_____

_____

_____

_____

WATER 🥤🥤🥤🥤🥤🥤🥤

EXERCISE

_____

_____

I AM GRATEFUL

THOUGHTS

LIVE FOR TODAY. DREAM ABOUT TOMORROW. BE GRATEFUL. LAUGH.

MAKING TODAY *Great!*

DATE:

AFFIRMATIONS ☐

MEDITATION ☐

READING ☐

SELF-CARE

CLOSER TO MY GOAL

HEALTHY EATING

WATER 🥛🥛🥛🥛🥛🥛🥛

EXERCISE

I AM GRATEFUL

THOUGHTS

LIVE FOR TODAY. DREAM ABOUT TOMORROW. BE GRATEFUL. LAUGH.

MAKING TODAY *Great!*

DATE: _____

AFFIRMATIONS ☐

MEDITATION ☐

READING ☐

SELF-CARE

CLOSER TO MY GOAL

HEALTHY EATING

WATER

EXERCISE

I AM GRATEFUL

THOUGHTS

LIVE FOR TODAY. DREAM ABOUT TOMORROW. BE GRATEFUL. LAUGH.

MAKING TODAY *Great!*

DATE:

AFFIRMATIONS ☐

MEDITATION ☐

READING ☐

SELF-CARE

CLOSER TO MY GOAL

HEALTHY EATING

WATER 🥛🥛🥛🥛🥛🥛🥛

EXERCISE

I AM GRATEFUL

THOUGHTS

LIVE FOR TODAY. DREAM ABOUT TOMORROW. BE GRATEFUL. LAUGH.

MAKING TODAY *Great!*

DATE: _____

AFFIRMATIONS ☐

MEDITATION ☐

READING ☐

SELF-CARE _____

CLOSER TO MY GOAL

_____

_____

_____

HEALTHY EATING

_____

_____

_____

_____

WATER 🥛🥛🥛🥛🥛🥛🥛

EXERCISE

_____

_____

I AM GRATEFUL

THOUGHTS

LIVE FOR TODAY. DREAM ABOUT TOMORROW. BE GRATEFUL. LAUGH.

MAKING TODAY *Great!*

DATE:

AFFIRMATIONS ☐

MEDITATION ☐

READING ☐

SELF-CARE

CLOSER TO MY GOAL

HEALTHY EATING

WATER 🥛🥛🥛🥛🥛🥛🥛

EXERCISE

I AM GRATEFUL

THOUGHTS

LIVE FOR TODAY. DREAM ABOUT TOMORROW. BE GRATEFUL. LAUGH.

MAKING TODAY *Great!*

DATE: _____

AFFIRMATIONS ☐

MEDITATION ☐

READING ☐

SELF-CARE

CLOSER TO MY GOAL

HEALTHY EATING

WATER 🥛🥛🥛🥛🥛🥛🥛

EXERCISE

I AM GRATEFUL

THOUGHTS

LIVE FOR TODAY. DREAM ABOUT TOMORROW. BE GRATEFUL. LAUGH.

MAKING TODAY *Great!*

DATE:

AFFIRMATIONS ☐

MEDITATION ☐

READING ☐

SELF-CARE

CLOSER TO MY GOAL

HEALTHY EATING

WATER 🥛🥛🥛🥛🥛🥛🥛

EXERCISE

I AM GRATEFUL

THOUGHTS

LIVE FOR TODAY. DREAM ABOUT TOMORROW. BE GRATEFUL. LAUGH.

MAKING TODAY *Great!*

DATE: _____

AFFIRMATIONS ☐

MEDITATION ☐

READING ☐

SELF-CARE _____

CLOSER TO MY GOAL

_____

_____

_____

HEALTHY EATING

_____

_____

_____

WATER 🥤🥤🥤🥤🥤🥤🥤

EXERCISE

I AM GRATEFUL

THOUGHTS

LIVE FOR TODAY. DREAM ABOUT TOMORROW. BE GRATEFUL. LAUGH.

MAKING TODAY *Great!*

DATE:

AFFIRMATIONS ☐

MEDITATION ☐

READING ☐

SELF-CARE

CLOSER TO MY GOAL

HEALTHY EATING

WATER 🥛🥛🥛🥛🥛🥛🥛

EXERCISE

I AM GRATEFUL

THOUGHTS

LIVE FOR TODAY. DREAM ABOUT TOMORROW. BE GRATEFUL. LAUGH.

MAKING TODAY *Great!*

DATE: _____

AFFIRMATIONS ☐

MEDITATION ☐

READING ☐

SELF-CARE _____

CLOSER TO MY GOAL

_____
_____
_____

HEALTHY EATING

_____
_____
_____

WATER 🥛🥛🥛🥛🥛🥛🥛

EXERCISE

_____

I AM GRATEFUL

THOUGHTS

LIVE FOR TODAY. DREAM ABOUT TOMORROW. BE GRATEFUL. LAUGH.

MAKING TODAY *Great!*

DATE:

AFFIRMATIONS ☐

MEDITATION ☐

READING ☐

SELF-CARE

CLOSER TO MY GOAL

HEALTHY EATING

WATER 🥛🥛🥛🥛🥛🥛🥛

EXERCISE

I AM GRATEFUL

THOUGHTS

LIVE FOR TODAY. DREAM ABOUT TOMORROW. BE GRATEFUL. LAUGH.

MAKING TODAY *Great!*

DATE: _____

AFFIRMATIONS ☐

MEDITATION ☐

READING ☐

SELF-CARE

CLOSER TO MY GOAL

HEALTHY EATING

WATER 🥛🥛🥛🥛🥛🥛🥛🥛

EXERCISE

I AM GRATEFUL

THOUGHTS

LIVE FOR TODAY. DREAM ABOUT TOMORROW. BE GRATEFUL. LAUGH.

MAKING TODAY *Great!*

DATE:

AFFIRMATIONS ☐

MEDITATION ☐

READING ☐

SELF-CARE

CLOSER TO MY GOAL

HEALTHY EATING

WATER 🥛🥛🥛🥛🥛🥛🥛

EXERCISE

I AM GRATEFUL

THOUGHTS

LIVE FOR TODAY. DREAM ABOUT TOMORROW. BE GRATEFUL. LAUGH.

MAKING TODAY *Great!*

DATE: _____

AFFIRMATIONS ☐

MEDITATION ☐

READING ☐

SELF-CARE _____

CLOSER TO MY GOAL

_____

_____

_____

HEALTHY EATING

_____

_____

_____

_____

WATER 🥤🥤🥤🥤🥤🥤🥤🥤

EXERCISE

_____

_____

I AM GRATEFUL

THOUGHTS

LIVE FOR TODAY. DREAM ABOUT TOMORROW. BE GRATEFUL. LAUGH.

Notes

Notes

Notes

Notes

Notes

Notes

Notes

Notes

Notes

Notes

Made in the USA
Middletown, DE
14 December 2018